SERMONS

FOR

CHRIST-LIKE

(CHRISTIAN)

LIVING

SERMONS

FOR

CHRIST-LIKE

(CHRISTIAN)

LIVING

DR. BOBBY E. MILLS

CONTENTS

Introduction 9

What Kind of Church Do You Want? 15

Doers of the Word of God 23

The Cost of Discipleship 31

What Think Ye of Jesus? 37

I Thirst: The Fifth Word 43

Freedom from Fear 51

The Suffering Servant 59

The Four P's of God 69

Caught Up and Can't Come Down 73

Fishers of Men 81

If a Man is Determined to be a Godly Father... 87

What Do You Do When it is Midnight? 97

What is Religion Doing to Your Character? 101

The Art of Forgetting 105

Christian Love 111

My God is So High You Can't Get Over Him 117

The Priority of Prayer 125

Conclusion 131

ACKNOWLEDGEMENTS

What we spiritually invest into the lives of others comes back into our own. My family invested a lot of spiritual, ethical, moral character capital into my development; especially my parents, grandparents, uncles and aunts, and for that spiritual investment, I am eternally thankful. To God be the glory!

Moreover, I especially thank my wife, Larnita, for her loving support throughout my college teaching career. I thank my son, Daryl Anthony, and my daughters, Kelly Leigh and Karen Rene`, for their love and devotion.

Grateful appreciation and heartfelt thanks and love are extended to Charles W. Moore, Dr. Robert E. Childress, Pastor Raymond L. Farley, Pastor John E. Cameron, and Pastor Kelly E. Reynolds. I love and thank you all. God's choice blessings forever and always!

INTRODUCTION

The greatness of God is usually experienced in loneliness. Every generation becomes wiser and wicked in the ways of the world and this is precisely why God needs Christians, especially in the twenty-first century, who are willing to boldly stand for righteousness' sake and resist the devil and evil.

God is not fickle-minded and neither was his only begotten Son, Jesus Christ, the Righteous One. More importantly, this is why Jesus foretold Peter's denial of him: "But Peter said unto him, although all shall be offended, yet will not I. And Jesus saith unto him, Verily I say unto thee, That this day, even in this night, before the cock crow twice, thou shall deny me thrice" (Mark 14:29-30). Hence, experiencing the holiness of God through the Spirit is why King David could boldly say: "Whom have I in heaven but thee? And there is none upon earth that I desire beside thee" (Psalms 73:25).

The greatest sermon ever preached came directly from Heaven and was preached by Jesus as "The Sermon on the Mount." The Beatitudes simply mean "Be of this Attitude." "And seeing the multitudes, he went up into a mountain: and when he was set, his disciples came unto him: and he opened his mouth, and taught them saying.

- Blessed are the poor in spirit: for theirs is the kingdom of Heaven. Blessed are they that mourn: for they shall be comforted.

- Blessed are the meek: for they shall inherit the earth.

- Blessed are they which do hunger and thirst after righteousness: for they shall be filled.

- Blessed are the merciful: for they shall obtain mercy. Blessed are the pure in heart: for they shall see God.

- Blessed are the peacemakers: for they shall be called the children of God.

- Blessed are they which are persecuted for righteousness' sake for theirs is the Kingdom of Heaven.

- Blessed are ye, when men shall revile you, and persecute you, and shall say all manner of evil against you falsely, for my sake. Rejoice, and be exceedingly glad: for great is your reward in heaven: for so persecuted they the prophets which were before you" (Matthew 5:1-12).

Preaching is about teaching as well as having the spiritual will to be an example of that which an individual teaches. Thus, preaching is spiritual instruction in the principles of God.

Jesus lived by the principles that he taught. This is why Jesus could boldly say, "If you do not believe me for what I say then follow me around and believe me for my works' sake." The most profound spiritual example of Jesus of practicing what he preached is the "Upper Room" example of Jesus washing the disciple's feet because they were mumbling and grumbling about who would be the greatest in the Kingdom.

"The Sermon On the Mount" is the greatest sermon that was ever preached, because it came from heaven. Of course, it did not take Jesus an extraordinarily long length of time to preach the Sermon on the Mount. The Bible states that Jesus sat and spiritually taught them not emotionalized them! Therefore, if pastoral leaders would only "study to shew thyself approved unto God, a workman that needeth not to be ashamed, rightly dividing the word of truth. But shun profane and vain babblings" (2 Timothy 2:15-16). More importantly, pastoral leaders must always remind themselves that "all scripture is given by inspiration of

God, and is profitable for doctrine, for reproof, for correction, for instruction in righteousness: that the man of God may be perfect, thoroughly furnished unto all good works" (2 Timothy 3:16-17).

In the twenty-first century, too many pastoral leaders are preaching and teaching material prosperity, a vulgar Gospel doctrine based upon personalized materialism "isms," rather than the Word of God and the spiritual principles of God. Luke 12:15 unequivocally declares, "Take heed, and beware of covetousness: for man's life consisteth not in the abundance of the things which he possesseth" (Luke 12:15). "Take heed" is a call to spiritual self-introspection (criticism). As a consequence, preaching in many instances has become entertainment rather than spiritual enlightenment.

It is a difficult time for twenty-first century Christianity and Christian service. "This know also, that in the last days perilous time shall come. For men shall be lovers of their own selves, covetous, proud, blasphemers, disobedient to parent, unthankful, unholy, without natural affection, trucebreakers, false accusers, incontinent, fierce, despisers of those that are good, traitors, heady, high-minded, lovers of pleasures more than lovers of God; having a form of godliness, but denying the power thereof: from such turn away" (2 Timothy 3:1-5).

Consequently, church attendance and family-life participation in church activities is dramatically down among twenty-first century millennials. Without a doubt, in order for the world to get right with God, the Christian church must get right and become the light of the world. Selah!

WHAT KIND OF CHURCH DO YOU WANT?

Scripture: James 1:22-27; James 1:5-8

We live in an age of spiritual-moral confusion. Many individuals are spiritually caught between their forward drive and their backward pull. The world is in a spiritual state of confusion because of the moral failure of the Christian leadership. The Christian church's moral failure is grounded in the social fact that too many church leaders are influenced by the world's culture, especially the entertainment aspect of church life. Rather than the church spiritually leading the world, the church is led by the world. In other words, the church is following after the material things of the world. The church is in the world, but should not be of the world. The Bible was written to the church, because of spiritual-moral-confusion in the church. Even in Biblical times, there was a lot of spiritual confusion and strife in the church. In fact, St. Paul's letters to the church were written about spiritual confusion in church life. There are two kinds of churches: (1) God's church and (2) the devil's church. The story is told of a little old lady on Halloween Night in a special church service. As a practical joke, a young parishioner dressed up in a devil's outfit and entered the church. Everyone quickly departed except one little old lady. The devil sat down beside her and asked: "Why aren't you afraid?" The little old lady answered, "I have been a member of this church for fifty years, and believe it or not, I have been on your side all the time!"

Let's be clear about one thing: God and institutional "religion" are not the same; likewise, God and church attendance are not the same. Here's the question Covenant Glen that I want you to consider today: What kind of church do you want? There are a lot of individuals who do not want any kind of church, and this is why they are at home in bed on Sunday mornings. Of course, there are those who attend church; simply because it is the socially, fashionable acceptable thing to do. These individuals are like the Pharisees; they simply want to be seen for their fine attire.

I am going to give you a formula for how we can have God's church where love works MIRACLES. First of all, let's clearly understand that "men build churches, women and children, and the elderly attend churches." Let me explain: God's church begins in the heart of an individual's mind (the invisible church); then the church is consummated institutionally in marriage in the family. It is spiritually written what God has joined together, let no man put asunder. Hence, marriage is about the church in the Home. Of course, the family that prays together stays together, because what God has put together no man can put asunder. The visible Church House on the street-corner is the Institutional Church which is made up of families. Who is the head of a family? When you have churches houses where men are not in attendance with their families you have broken churches. Broken churches reflect broken families, and broken families create broken communities, and dysfunctional societies.

Broken communities create a broken nation state, and broken nations create a broken morally confused world community. Moreover, we have too many "Witch Doctor Pastors" breaking up families by preaching the Gospel of Prosperity as though family is an economic unit, rather than a spiritual unit. God is not a divine Santa Claus. One well-known-pastor had 1700 divorces in one year in the church he pastors. Thus, his preaching of material prosperity literally broke up 1700 families.

The Formula for Having God's Church

To have God's church, you must first "go to church before you come to church." Individuals must bring sacredness (Spiritual Meaning) to church houses, not worldly carnality. If you go to church before you come to church then you will understand the spiritual meaning of church. By all means, remember the church begins in the heart of an individual's mind and is made sacred in the family. The primary role of church is to help make your family life more creatively religious. Ask the average church goer, "What was the message from the sermon they just heard?" They could not tell you; but ask them about the choir/singing, and you'll receive an ear full. Therefore, if you go to church before you come to church you will understand church attendance, because the Book of Corinthians reminds us that "you" are the church.

Second, the church is a hospital for the spiritually sick, and therefore, the church must know how to repair lives (Spiritual Healing). The church must know how to restore those in the FAITH who have slipped/fallen in their Christian walk with God, for all have sinned and fallen short of what God expects of us. Those of us without SIN; cast the first stone. The church must re-enforce the importance of "positive scriptural self-talk." For, what does it profit an individual to gain the whole world and lose his soul? A person's life does not consist in the abundance of things which he possesses. The love of money is the root of all evil (1 Timothy 6:10). John 8:31-32: "If you continue in my Word, then you are my Disciples," and "you shall know the Truth and the Truth shall make you free," The only way a church can repair lives is by helping individuals understand the principles of God. Of course, the principles of God are not popular. Hebrews 5:12 says, "For when for the time ye ought to be teachers,

Ye have need that one teach you again which be the first principles of the Oracles of God; and are become such as have need of milk, and not strong meat. For everyone that needs MILK is unskillful in the Word of Righteousness: for he is a babe."

The Purpose of Church is to Repair Lives Spiritually

The purpose of Church is to repair lives so that individuals might clearly understand the Plan of God Job 7:17-18: "What is man that thou should magnify him?" Hebrews 2:6:

"What is man that thou art mindful of him?" God's plan for us is that we should be witnesses for the TRUTH. For the purpose of God is that individuals should glorify Him. God must receive the glorify and as His children, we should honor one another by loving and serving each other. The Two Great Commandments: "Thou shalt love the Lord thy God with all thy heart, and with all thy mind. This is the first and great commandment. And the second is like unto it, Thou shalt love thou neighbor as thyself. On these two commandments hang all the law and the prophets" (Matthew 22:37-40). Therefore, when we abide in God's principles, understand God's Salvation Plan, and embrace God's purpose for our lives we receive salvation for our souls. It is then that an individual can let the Light of his or her life so shine that individuals might see their good works and their work will glorify our Heavenly Father.

The Real Meaning of Church is Learning to Share

Last, after you learn to go to church before you come to church, and while in church, you learn how to repair lives and strengthen lives; now you are ready to share the love of God that was in Christ Jesus reconciling the world unto God and us unto each other. This is a spiritually precise interpretation of the Great Commission. The church has been commissioned to transform the world, not to be transformed by the world. "For God so loved the world that He gave his only begotten Son, for whosoever believeth in Him should not perish but have eternal life," (John 3:16). Go in through the narrow gate, for wide is the gate and broad is the road; which leads to ruin, and there are many who go in through it. But, narrow is the gate and hard is the way that leads to eternal life, and those who find it are few. God says I have set before you this day, life and good, and death and evil. Choose (life and good) so that your seed might live. Today, too many of our children are lawless (spiritually-lost), and therefore, they do not have knowledge of the lawgiver—GOD." Far too many parents are not sharing the love of God that was in Jesus Christ; reconciling us unto God and individuals unto each other. It is a spiritual imperative that the church gets right with God, because America's spiritual-moral walls have been torn down. Amen and thank God!

DOERS OF THE WORD OF GOD

Scripture: James 1:19-27

But be ye doers of the Word. John 1:1 says: "In the beginning was the Word, and the Word was with God, and the Word was God." In the beginning was the TRUTH. The Truth was with God, and the Truth was God. All things came into being by the Truth and apart from Truth nothing came into being.

Now, think with me: **every human being is conceived as God's truth, because truth belongs to God.** So, what turns an individual into the devil's lie or lies? A lie belongs to the devil. Truth creates and a lie destroys. The word devil simply means evil mind. What makes an individual evil is his or her WILL; hence, if an individual wills to do evil, he becomes an agent of the devil. If an individual wills to be righteous, that is, to do good, he is a child of God. This is why James admonishes us to

"Be doers of the Word/Truth", because truth creates life and life more abundantly.

Second, James admonishes us to be mindful of the fact that anger does not achieve the righteousness of God. Anger arises out of hatred or contempt toward others, because anger is a classic clash of wills. God's righteousness is impartial. His justice includes all. God makes His rain to fall on the just and the unjust alike. God is not arbitrary. God is not arrogant. God is not vindictive. Hence, James reminds us that the religion of an individual ought to cause him to bridle his tongue and control his temper. If your religion does not cause you to bridle your tongue, then it is empty pretense, and you have become a great pretender. Of course, there is a form of righteous anger that individuals are justified in having. (Mark 3:5). That anger is when an individual expresses public resentment against actions which cause others to suffer without blame on their part. Someone once said, "I do well to be angry at times, but I usually chose the wrong times." More importantly, "God judgeth the righteous, and God is angry with the wicked every day," (Psalm 7:11).

Third, Christian worship is not designed for God, but for human beings. God does not have to be psyched or cajoled into being gracious. The difficulty is not with God, but with individuals. It is the spiritual response of people that is hard to obtain. God always responds. Individuals have to be brought to the persuasion of God's love to receive with meekness divine instruction. To worship God in "Spirit and Truth," individuals must be willing to cleanse their hearts and minds of all worldly filthiness. First Peter 1:16 says, "You shall be Holy, for I am Holy." Here is the spiritual point that James was attempting to make: the practical value of church attendance is only realized when the Truth heard becomes the Truth in action. Pious worship followed by unethical actions is damnation to the Soul. In all of His teachings and daily living, Jesus sought to sensitize the conscience of individuals to the will of God. Moreover, before God can speak to an individual, He must be able to command the attention of that person. God demands that we should listen, and God demands that we should act in love.

Fourth, James wants us to know that the Truth of God is like a "two-edged sword." It cuts both ways. It hurts the teller as well as the receiver. Some church members slack in church attendance, because they do not want to expose themselves to God's truth. Trust me the Truth of God will disturb your moral and spiritual complacency. Someone once said that what is wrong with the Christian church is that individuals sitting in the pews Sunday after Sunday need to be converted. That is, there are too many Christians who have become God's frozen people. Too many Christians are simply benchwarmers. Thus, the JESUSWAY is the only path to spiritual freedom. The law of God for James does not negate freedom, but gives freedom. The law of God does not place a limitation upon living; it simply points individuals in the right direction in which life must flow. Restlessness, frustration, despair, and dissatisfaction are not the issues of a servant of God, but they are the issues of rebels against God.

Fifth, according to James, pure religion is devotion to God demonstrated by compassionate relationships with our fellowman. What doth the LORD require of thee: "BUT TO DO JUSTLY, AND TO LOVE MERCY, AND TO WALK HUMBLY WITH GOD" (Micah 6:8). Pure religion is about ethics. Pure religion is about saying what you mean and meaning what you say. Pure religion is about living by every word that comes out of your mouth because if individuals are not willing to live by words that come out of their own mouth, they certainly will not live by words in the Bible. Hence, pure religion is about ordering your steps by the Word of God. Pure religion is about elevating your thoughts to a higher plain. Pure religion is about taking inventory of your life. Pure religion is about asking the question: HOW

DO I LIVE? But, more importantly, what am I willing to sacrifice so that I can live the way I say I want to live? Redemptive suffering. James, just like Jesus, urges us to be what we are for each other, because being what we are is to be what God wants us to be in Him. In so doing, we have God's assurance that works of the Spirit lead to eternal life. Jesus came to reconcile individuals unto each other and individuals unto God. The life of Jesus was to the glory of God. This is why James invites us to get our values straight so that our lives might spiritually glorify God. When we get our values straight we will be able not just to see the beginning, but we will be able to spiritually see the end of the way towards eternal life; that is, we will see things not in the light of time, but in the light of eternity.

The price tag on Christ-likeness is high, because individuals must forego many roads to walk the straight and narrow road. Great living or "low-life-living" entails self-sacrifice. To be sure, one never really gets something for nothing. When individuals desire something for nothing; invariably they get nothing, and nothing from nothing leaves nothing. Life isn't that simple. It is for this reason alone that Jesus talks about "counting the cost." "Pay as you enter. Pay as you leave. Or, fly now and pay later. But, sooner or later pay you must. In short, you pay for the ride you chose."

Lastly, James exhorts us, our being, that is, our being what we are, is our actively being involved in the Community of grace—the Christian church. This is the fellowship of Christians in the world. And, of course, we are constantly being called to participate in the power of God through the JESUSWAY. Thank God for the life of Jesus!

As Christians, we are called to a life of fullness and eternal happiness. But, we do not always hear the cry of God, because our spirits have been mummified to the will of God. The command that we love each other is often ignored, but the charge of Jesus is always before us: "COME FOLLOW ME AND I WILL MAKE YOU FISHERS OF MEN." That is, I will teach you how to save lives so that we fail not ourselves and our children, as well as future generations, which in turn, is our physical immortality knowing full well that God can do anything We should be who we are in Christ; therefore, let us pledge today and everyday that we will become like James, a faithful doer of the Word/Truth, for, when this happens through faith, hope, and love (charity), we can bear each other's burdens and so fulfill the law of Jesus Christ: love God and love your neighbor as yourself.

LET US PRAY: O God, strengthen our spiritual weaknesses that we may do well in our spiritual warfare battle. Help us against our cowardice; bestow upon us Thy courage that we might be able to face the challenges of life, and never fail to think brave thoughts, and to do brave deeds through the love of Jesus Christ. Amen!

THE COST OF DISCIPLESHIP: THE RHETORIC OF A ROOSTER

Scripture: Matthew 4:18-22

For Jesus, community was the unquestioned presupposition of human life. Jesus walked along the shores of the Galilee River calling men out of their occupations and preoccupations with themselves, to form a community under the sovereignty of God.

Jesus had just been baptized in the Jordan River by John the Baptist, and for forty days and nights He had prayed and fasted in the wilderness. Of course, He was constantly tempted by the devil. Immediately, after the wilderness experience Jesus began His ministry with a call: "COME FOLLOW ME, AND I WILL MAKE YOU FISHERS OF MEN." Jesus called men out of themselves to spiritually remake their lives. This call was revolutionary in the lives of Andrew and Simon Peter. They repented, they denied themselves, and they followed Jesus. In speaking to them, Jesus spoke beyond them to future generations who would have an ear to listen, and a mind/heart to follow. But, just like most of us, the (12) disciples did not fully count the cost of discipleship. Yes, there is a high price tag on following after righteousness. Hence, Christ is a title that means the "Righteous One." So to follow after Christ is to follow after righteousness.

Peter was arrogant and self-righteous enough to believe that he had it all together, because he thought he knew exactly what it meant to be a disciple of righteousness. In Matthew 26:30-35, Jesus forecasted Peter's denial of Him letting him know that the rhetoric of a rooster, the sounds of nothingness would call him out, because before the rooster crows, Peter would deny Him three times. Of course, "the tough the do not always get going; sometimes they flee the scene mentally and even physically".

Discipleship is costly (Luke.14:.25-35). Jesus says, if any man comes after Me, he must hate father, mother, sister, brother, even his own life, or he cannot be My disciple. Discipleship requires three distinct types of commitments:

(1) Self-Denial. Deny all for the sake of the Kingdom of God, because Kingdom building requires total commitment (Chicken and Pig story). Discipleship is a call to spend one's life in service to God and others.

(2) Cross-Bearing. Here Jesus indicates that every man has a cross to bear and a burden to carry. No man can die for another, so no man can carry another's cross. Each individual is responsible for his own life under God's Sovereignty. The idea that there is a cross for everyone to bear caused a lot of friction between Jesus and His disciples. Jesus calls individuals to make a commitment to life, not death. Remember the man who Jesus issued the called to: "And He replied, my father just died, I'll follow you, but first let me go back home and bury him." Jesus' reply was "let the dead bury the dead." Remember the man who wanted to go back home and say goodbye to his loved ones: "And Jesus replied once you put your hands to the plow you cannot look back." Life is about looking ahead, not looking back. There was a spiritual power in Jesus' call to discipleship, because it has the power to liberate individuals from old relationships with self to a new relationship with God and one's neighbor. Jesus' call has the power to free us to become the New Being in Christ

(3) **Dailiness of the job.** Discipleship is not an occasional or sometime job but a full-time responsibility that requires the wholehearted commitment of one's life to the truth of God, not the lies of the devil. A disciple must remain on the job, twenty-four/seven, for no man knoweth the hour or the day when the watchman cometh. A disciple cannot be like John and James who thought that to follow Jesus meant sitting on His right hand in the Kingdom of God. Jesus had to remind them that to follow Him meant cross-bearing.

Today, the challenge that was issued two thousand years ago comes to you and me as Christian believers. "Come Follow Me And Learn Of God." The first disciples were not men of great scholarship, or social influence, or even great wealth, or high social status. They did not have successful career futures according to the standards of the world. They were common ordinary men. All they had to offer to the cause of Jesus Christ was themselves, that is, devoted lives. Too many Christians have become God's frozen people." We are pew-warmers / bench-warmers. We cannot and dare not become fishers of men, that is, evangelize souls for God. Moreover, we do not know how to become a light post for God, and let our lights so shine that men might see God in our works, but, more importantly, create in individuals a desire to come running and saying, "What must I do to be saved?"

Four Keys to Becoming Fishers of Men

1. **PATIENCE.** We must learn to wait upon God. One never witnesses quick results in teaching and preaching. One must be willing to try, try, and try again.

2. **COURAGE.** Individuals must be ready and willing to face all kinds of dangers, for there is always a danger in telling individuals the truth. More often than not, the person who tells the truth takes his life in his hands in a world that hates the truth.

3. **AN EYE FOR THE RIGHT MOMENT.** A wise fisherman knows that it is hopeless to fish sometimes; therefore, an individual must know when to cast and when not to cast. He must choose his moment wisely. There are times when people will welcome the truth, and there are times when they will resent the truth. There is a time to speak and a time to be silent.

4. **FITTING THE BAIT TO THE FISH.** Some individuals will accept the Word of God, and others will reject it. A wise fisherman knows that he will win some, and he will lose

some. St. Paul said it best: "I became all things to all men so that by chance I might win a few."

As Christians, we must present individuals with the TRUTH at all cost, because the life of Jesus was about the TRUTH OF GOD.

Today, I challenge you to hitch your wagon to a star, and that star must lead you to the Cross and ultimately to the call of Jesus to CHRISTIAN DISCIPLESHIP.

For it was at the Cross that truth was crushed to the ground, but three days later, it rose again even more victorious. Today, truth issues a clarion call: "Come follow Me and I will teach you how to save souls." This is our "Call", because every

Christian believers are called to embrace the ministry of Jesus Christ, and to love and serve others rather than to seek self-service. A Christian's desire must be to console rather than to seek consolation; that is, to minister to the needy in the name of God's TRUTH. Jesus is calling, today, and if you answer His call, He will show you the path of life wherein PEACE, LOVE, and JOY ABIDE. Must Jesus bear the Cross alone and all the world go free? No, there is a Cross for everyone. There is a cross for you and a cross for me. God bless you this day and every day, henceforth and evermore. Amen!

WHAT THINK YE OF JESUS, THE SON OF THE LIVING GOD?

Scripture: Matthew 22:42

Jesus asked the Pharisees and Sadducees this question: "What think ye of Christ? Whose son is he?" (Matthew 22:42).

What do you make of Jesus the Christ? Sooner or later every discussion of religion leads to this question! Sooner or later, in some manner, all of us are going to run up against the life of Jesus as a measuring rod. Our individual answers may be different from the church's answer. Many have called Jesus a prophet or poet; some have even called him a great teacher, and He has even been called a psychologist. The question today is: what is your opinion of Jesus the Christ? Now, think with me. Jesus Himself thought that this was an important question. Therefore, the question is an inescapable one because it is an eternal question. Every individual has an interest in Jesus though he may not even be aware of it. There are some who know but simply do not care. Without a doubt, apart from Jesus, human life can never be what God intended it to be. St. Peter was asked this question by Jesus: "Whom do men say that I am," and Peter answered by saying: "Thou art Christ, the Son of the Living God." Jesus replied by saying that flesh and blood did not reveal this to Peter. Hence, the Christian tradition has eternalized the life of Jesus, and therefore, Jesus becomes the measure of individual as well as collective humanity. Jesus is the eternal standard of measurement for what we are and for what Christianity can be or for what it is.

Jesus belongs to the world, and as Christians, we belong to Jesus. Because of Jesus's obedience to God, He was given a name above all names (CHRIST). The use of the title CHRIST assures us that Jesus is victorious. The title Christ means "The Righteous One." God was in Jesus reconciling the world unto Him. In trusting ourselves in God's care, we meet Jesus through the action of the Holy Spirit. For if any individual is in Christ (Righteousness) he is a new creature; he is a new being. Moreover, he has a new relationship with almighty God.

Jesus is what is new, and Jesus is what is old. Individuals have always sought to understand the meaning of life, and Jesus comes to teach us what things are true and just. To live life creatively you must have a spiritual rendezvous with Jesus. Have you had a rendezvous with Jesus? Have you met Jesus at the crossroads of life? Have you met Jesus in the Garden? Every individual at some point in his or her life must come to grips with the meaning of the life of Jesus—not how Jesus died, but how He lived. Jesus did not die on the cross, but He died in the will of God. Therefore, if we live the way Jesus lived, and we die where He died, in the will of God, we have everlasting life. Jesus was the bearer of the Kingdom of God. His ethic is that of the New Age and the New Covenant. He is the agent of God. Jesus used God as the model for His life: "Be ye perfect as your father in heaven is perfect." God demands perfection from all of us, that is, perfection in His will. You can be perfect. You are perfect when you realize the reason for your creation.

Jesus said there are two things a man must have: (1) an awareness of God and (2) faith because faith pleases God. Faith is the action by which an individual helps to create an encounter with God.

Jesus is the absolute proclaimer of the will of God. God stepped down in Jesus so that He might step up in us. We are always stepping up and stepping on others by fooling ourselves into believing that this is the way to get ahead in the world. But,

Jesus says he who seeks to save shall lose, but he who is willing to lose for the sake of the Kingdom of God shall find. Jesus says, I am meek and lowly of heart, and my burden is light, come unto me, and you shall find rest for your souls.

Shall you and I commit the fatal mistake of letting Jesus tread the pages of history as just a good guy? Or, do we proclaim Him as the standard of measurement for our lives? I ask you today . . .

Are you wearing the right clothes? The clothing of Jesus is not a reference to outward physical appearance. Jesus is not talking about physical clothes that come from Macy's, Saks 5th Avenue, Neiman Marcus, or any other high-end-clothing store. Nor is Jesus talking about clothing with designer labels. Jesus is referencing the heart of an individual's mind and his motives, his inner spirit, not his outward physical appearance. So, Jesus asks this question: *Are you wearing the right clothes?* Do you have on the breastplate of righteousness and the helmet of your salvation? My Christian friends, you can only experience the company (presence) and friendship of Jesus when you wear the right clothing. God gives us His robe of righteousness and the garments of gratitude and gladness. We should be glad because God accepts us even though we rebel against Him. Of course, in rebellion, we become rebels without a cause. For it is a certainty that every individual has a spiritual appointment with the living God, and therefore, you had best become extremely careful about the clothing you wear. What do you think of Jesus is the question? And, the clothes that you wear will define your answer. I pray that Jesus' style of living has become your style, and in so doing you help to make the world a better-more-loving-place (Peace on earth and good will toward all). Amen and thank God for His grace, mercy, and ever loving kindness.

I THIRST: THE FIFTH WORD

The seven statements that Jesus made during the hours of His death depict the humanity of Jesus. Jesus was a man who was willing to spend Himself and to be spent in every way for others.

Jesus, like most human beings, did not want to accept the ultimate in life, which in turn, is physical death. Of course, it is only in that individuals truly understand the spiritual meaning of physical death do they begin to spiritually understand the true meaning of life.

Obviously, the fifth word has more symbolic meaning than just the physiological fact that Jesus was thirsty for a drink of cool water. Jesus was also thirsty for liberation from physical pain as well as the body of death that confronted Him. Like St. Paul, Jesus was saying: "O wretched man that I am, who will save me from this body of death?" which in turn, was evident in

His statement: "My God, my God, why hast thou forsaken me?" (Matthew 27:46).

Thus, Jesus, in His humanity, wanted deliverance from the vicissitudes of life. He wanted some assurance that His life was not going to be snuffed out in the world as it is, or the world as it shall be in the future. It was in His despair that Jesus realized that the only trustworthy force in the world as we know it is Almighty God.

Peter had denied Him. Judas had betrayed Him. Jesus came to His own, and they had not received Him nor accepted Him.

Jesus was in despair, and He wanted to renege on the commitment. "Father if it be Thy will, take this bitter cup of death from me." But, God in the midst of death liberated Jesus from His fears and moved His vision to a higher plain; so that you and I might be spiritually reconciled unto God as well as unto each other.

The devil brought confusion into the human family, and Jesus comes as the reconciler and liberator for those of us who will receive the Good News of the Gospel.

In other words, the ministry of Jesus even unto death was one of liberation and reconciliation. Jesus called men out of themselves and out of their selfishness to become new beings, who are a force for positive good. This was an urgent call. This call does not have time-barriers, because it transcends time and embraces eternity. Individuals do not have time to say goodbye to a loved one, or even bury a dead father. Once you put your hands to the plough there can be no looking back or turning around.

Of course, there is a huge difference between real and ideal commitment.

Real commitment is a bread and butter issue. Ideal commitment is a cross-bearing issue. In other words, God demands unquestioning loyalty that is the kind of loyalty that will lead you to a burden that you alone must bear and a cross that only you must bear.

God demands commitment unto death. When God calls, individuals must "take the high road home," because there are no short-cuts to eternal life, the Kingdom of Heaven.

Therefore, Jesus has called us to become reconcilers and liberators. What, then, does it mean to be a reconciler and a liberator? It means that we should become advocates for love, justice, and spiritual power.

Jesus has left us the instrument to accomplish this mission; it is His church, not our church. The question becomes:

What kind of church do you want? Perhaps there are some of us who don't want any kind of church, simply because we do not understand the importance of church attendance (fellowship); hence, there are many who stay home on a Sunday morning, and their prayer is: "Give me this day my day in bed."

However, the chances are you want the church to be at her best.

Of course, if you have grown impatient with the church, and you have been let down by the church or some church member(s), know this: you don't stay away from the movie theater or sporting events because one movie was lousy or your favorite team lost the game.

When church property is unkempt, it does not mean that church members are poor. It simply means that they don't care very much.

The church we belong to should point away from itself toward others. We go to church to worship, but we must also serve. An individual's church must be a church that spiritually educates. When we worship, we keep an appointment with God, and that appointment is that we have been called to serve the world.

Just like Saint Paul, we must say, 'I appeal to you brethren, to present yourselves before God as a living sacrifice, holy, acceptable, and good, which is your spiritual worship.'

The truth of the church is not soothing. It can be highly explosive, and it should be. Many of our beliefs and attitudes about church should be blown apart, and of course, they should be!

What kind of church do you want? Do you want a church that spiritualizes or emotionalizes? Do you want a church that deals with the collective social needs of the community or a church that turns inward to self-serve? Do you want a church that deals with your personal hang-ups? Jesus' ministry was one of mission to cast out the demons in society.

Too many church-goers want a feel-good -religion that comforts them in their mess, but does not challenge them in their existence and daily living. For it is only a fool who beholds his natural face in the mirror and then walks away forgetting the image that he has seen? The Black church from its inception was a socio-political-economic institution that dealt with the inhumanity of "Institutional Racism". In many instances, Black churches have turned away from this historical tradition to one of solely giving emotional comfort; that is, a Sunday kind of feel-good religious experience that ends when the worship service ends.

We should want a church that can give us the kind of religion that we can take with us Monday thru Saturday, and moreover, apply it in our daily living.

How many of us here have been resurrected with Jesus? How many of us have been down with Jesus for a little while and then up for eternity? How many of us are willing to deal with the social ills that Jesus dealt with: to feed the hungry, to clothe the naked, to take care of the homeless, and visit the sick and shut-in?

Too many individuals think that the cross meant defeat, but to God it was victory. Jesus is too great for small hearts and minds, and therefore, we cannot hold Him, because He shows us stars we have not seen before. For every individual's wagon must be hitched to a star, and that star must lead him to the foot of the cross whereby we can boldly say: "Must Jesus bear the Cross alone and all the world go free? No, there is a Cross for everyone, including thee." The resurrection is not a fact for historians to intellectually debate. It is a place for individuals who want somewhere to stand to take a stand for righteousness sake. It is at the foot of the cross where individuals are given the power to become the new being in Christ that is the power for an individual to be for others.

Yes, whenever we lay the scene, Jesus always comes back. Since that Friday, when they buried Him in a borrowed tomb, the Spirit of Jesus comes back in the lives of men like Martin Luther King, Jr., John F. Kennedy, Robert F. Kennedy, and Lyndon B. Johnson.

When individuals fail to understand that their limitations are not God's limitations they miss the importance of creatively living life. Moreover, when we fail that doesn't mean that God has failed because God can do anything but fail. It only means that we failed ourselves as well as God.

It is not easy to be like Jesus. M.L.K., J.F.K., and R.F.K. attempted to do so. Of course, it requires a commitment unto death. Too many of us are like Pontius Pilate. We wash our hands and call it quits, and say let the record stand. We might always have poverty, war, and sin, because there will always be some individuals who aren't willing to set examples of spiritual-moral-character for others to live by; therefore, they say, "Let the record stand."

So that you fail not God and yourselves, let us thirst for spiritual reconciliation as well as social liberation, that kind of liberation that makes us into the right kind of stuff as well as the kind of liberation that makes our churches into the right kind of stuff; the kind of liberation that teaches us to become advocates for love, justice, and power. Therefore, let us commit to being what it is that God has called us to be in His service to each other and for each other in Jesus' name. Amen and thank God!

FREEDOM FROM FEAR: THE KING'S MESSAGE TO THE DISCIPLES

Scripture: Matthew 10:26-28

"For there is nothing which is covered which shall not be unveiled and there is nothing hidden which shall not be known. What I tell you in the darkness, speak in the light. What you hear whispered in your ear, proclaim on the house tops. Do not fear those who can kill the body, but who cannot kill the soul. Rather, fear him who is able to destroy body and soul in Gehenna. Are not two sparrows not sold for a half-penny, and not one of them shall light on the ground without your father's knowledge? The hairs of your head are all numbered. So, then, be not afraid you are of more value than many sparrows."

Three times in this short passage Jesus bids His disciples not to be afraid. In Jesus' message, there was a certain courageous fearlessness that set Him apart from other men.

The first commandment is in Matthew 10:26-27, and it speaks of a double fearlessness. The disciples are not to be afraid because there is nothing covered that will not be unveiled, and nothing hidden which will not be known. The meaning of this is very clear: "The truth will triumph."

When King James VI threatened to hang or exile Andrew Melville who was a great English pastoral leader, Melville answered by saying: "You cannot hang or exile the truth." You can kill the body, but you cannot kill the truth. A Christian must know that suffering has a redemptive quality about it. For if a Christian suffers for the sake of righteousness, his suffering-deeds will be judged in the light of eternity, not in the light of time. What Jesus told His disciples, they must tell others! For after all, in this one verse (verse 27), lies the true function of preachers of the Gospel of Good News. The preacher must tell the truth at all costs. But, before he can tell the truth, he must first listen to God, because listening is a *godly* quality.

No man can speak for Jesus unless God has first spoken to him. No man can proclaim the truth of God unless he has first listened to the truth. No individual can tell that which he does not know. How can a man warm the coldness of others when he is shivering on the inside himself? A preacher must speak what he has received from God even if his speaking gains him the hatred of individuals. Individuals, indeed, love lies more so than the truth. There was a great preacher by the name of Latimer who was preaching. King Henry was present. Latimer knew that he was about to say something that would certainly offend the King, so from the pulpit he cried aloud: "Latimer! Latimer! Latimer! Be careful what you say. Henry the King is here, today." Then, he paused momentarily and said: "Latimer! Latimer! Latimer! Be careful of what you say. The King of Kings is here, today." The man with a message must speak the truth to others because when he speaks, he must recognize that he is speaking in the presence of God. At all costs pastoral leaders must preach and teach the principles of God, in and out, of season. For whether we teach or preach, we must teach and preach the principles of God.

It was said of John Knox as they buried him: "Here lies one who feared God so much that he never feared the face of any man." A Christian minister must listen with reverence and speak with boldness the truth of God, for whether he listens or speaks; he is always in the presence of God. This is why preaching is not social entertainment but spiritual enlightenment. Preaching is not whooping, but rightfully dividing the Word of truth."

There are three elements that are necessary for learning how to live free from fear. You have nothing to fear is the King of Kings message. It has rightly been said, Individuals, ultimately, have nothing to fear but fear itself.

(1) PERSONAL FAITH. Faith pertains to all of life, not just religion. Just as one cannot separate the love of God from the love of self, so it is with faith. You cannot separate faith in God from faith in self.

In this passage of Scripture (Matthew 10: 26-28), Jesus was telling His disciples, yes, it is true: men can kill your physical body, but God can condemn a man's soul to an eternal death. The Jews knew the awfulness of the punishment of God. The fear of God is the beginning of wisdom. There is a difference between holy fear and unholy fear. Disloyalty to God is worse than physical death. If a man is guilty of disloyalty to God he buys physical security at the expense of dishonor, and life is no longer tolerable. There are times when comfort ease, physical security, and the good life can cost too much. God cares for us, so we have no need for unholy fear. We can trust God. Our faith in God is never misdirected. If God cares for the sparrows, surely He will care for you, (Matthew 10:31). Above all, keep the faith because faith pleases God.

(2) PATIENCE. We must run this Christian race in patience and genuine love. Love is having great patience. God is patiently waiting for each one of His children to find his or her way back home. Be of good cheer. Be patience. Wait until your change comes. Don't think that you should have everything you want, right now. Instant gratification is a dangerous commodity! Be careful. There is instant gratification benefits in sin, otherwise individuals would not sin. To know love is to know self, and perfect love has no fears. Run, run, run this Christian race with patience for the race is not given to the swift, but to the one who endures to the end. Don't be too quick to point the finger, for the last time the finger is pointed, it will be towards you.

(3) MAKING YOU YOUR BEST FRIEND. God wants you to be your best friend, because just maybe if you are your best friend, you will always have a friend. Thus, with bold confidence an individual can sing: "What a friend we have in Jesus." Of course, the meaning of "what a friend we have in

Jesus" is simply this: Jesus was a friend to everyone, but who was a friend to Jesus? So it is with you and me: we can be a friend to others, but that does not guarantee that they will be our friend. If you are your best friend then you will be God's friend, because the question is: "Who is on the Lord's side?"

However, the devil wants you to become your worst enemy. The objective of the devil is to convince individuals to become their own enemy. One of the many ways the devil gets us to become our own enemy is by getting us to place money values over spiritual-moral values. The devil is the father of this world, and one of his instruments of power is money. This is why the Bible declares "For the love of money is the root of all evil: which while some coveted after; that have erred from the faith, and pierced themselves through with many sorrows" (1 Timothy 6:10). If we place money values above spiritual-moral values, then we get caught between our forward drive and our backward pull. And, we don't know whether we should look higher or look lower. Of course, the higher individuals look the more spiritual insight they gain about the reality of God. A good example of this is Ezekiel's wheel in the middle of a wheel experience (Ezekiel 1:16). We deny the truth with our words and deeds. And, we deny the truth with our silence by refusing to speak the truth in love. Therefore, go not where the path may lead, but go instead where there is no path and blaze a trail. Be a trail blazer! I leave you with this paradox: If you think about others first, you will learn to be selfish, but if you think about yourself first, you will learn to be generous. Think about it on your way home! God bless you and yours in the name of Jesus' Christ! Amen!

THE SUFFERING SERVANT

"But he was wounded for our transgressions; he was bruised for our iniquities: the chastisement of our peace was upon him; and with his stripes we are healed. All we like sheep have gone astray; we have turned everyone to his own way, and the Lord hath laid on him the iniquity of us all." (Isaiah 53: 5-7).

Our text is part of the suffering servant songs which was written during the closing days of the exiles in Babylonia. The exiles were uprooted, were avoided, and were social outcasts. In fact, they were despised even by their own kind. But, by the very means of their suffering they brought healing to others as well as to themselves. The exiles had no power, they had no prestige, they were separated from their homeland, and the Holy Temple was no more. But, they had learned that they had inner spiritual resources far more rewarding than external material growth from without. They used their energies by participating in life creatively, and taking an optimistic view of life; they triumphed over personal tragedy. Indeed, they were an example of character for others to imitate. Their standards and spiritual-moral values lay not were moth and rust do corrupt, nor where thieves break through and steal. In fact, they became a lamp unto the feet for some and a lighted pathway for others. To be sure, suffering leads to a ministry to others as well as a priceless lesson and heritage in thought and conduct.

Let's take a look at their formula. Spiritual development among the Greeks can be expressed in the spiritual formula from myth to logic or systematized knowledge. Here, an individual can stand apart from one's words or thoughts. But, for the Hebrews, spiritual development can be expressed in the formula from myth to logos or systematized knowledge. In fact, "The Word became flesh and dwelt among us and we beheld its glory." The thoughts of the exiles in Babylonia became a part of their flesh, and through their flesh they have left a profound lesson, not only in thought, but in moral conduct. "And with their stripes we are healed. All we like sheep have gone astray; and the Lord has laid on them the iniquity of us all". They were oppressed, afflicted, and yet, they bore the sins of many.' It is no surprise that the Christian church has traditionally interpreted the cross of Jesus in this context. For both the servant and Jesus, suffering is the means whereby they fulfill their mission and bring it to a triumphant conclusion.

What happened to the servant or the people in our text can happen to us as individuals. Suffering is the common lot of us all, and all the devices of individuals are unable to make us immune to suffering. Sooner or later suffering touches us all in some manner or another. The question then is not whether we will suffer, but when? The question then becomes how will we interpret and transform our suffering into spiritual redemption? Here, the Scripture lesson is emphatically clear and the spiritual lesson is priceless. We can take a bright view of life that will overcome our hidden wounds, damaged egos, and personal defeats. When this happens, we will have won the invisible victory. Or, on the other hand, we can take a defeatist and pessimistic attitude toward life. It's sad to see the face of a person confronting personal tragedy. Yet, if an individual keeps his courage and faith, personal tragedy can be overcome. But, you must keep your inner spirit and your inner courage. This is what happened to the exiles in our text. Perhaps, all of us know how it feels to gamble and lose. Rewards of all kinds pass us by.

It is in such moments that we must not let our moral courage escape us. The people of our text turned suffering into opportunity over against disaster. They had no army, but they had the power of redemptive suffering. Make no mistake about it, suffering is real, and I am not recommending by any means or measure that anyone take a course in suffering. But we are asserting the empirical social reality that no individual is an island unto himself. All of us are caught up in this business of living life daily, and the time has come for us to engage in serious conversation about the issue of suffering. Then, no one will have to say, "We have turned each one to his own way."

The idea or practice that everyone can go his or her own way is not only misleading, it is extremely dangerous, as well. Everything in God's creation operates according to some law or principle. And, this idea or practice that everyone can go his own way has no place or authority where a common goal or cause is the issue. In fact, there is no genuine own way. All ways are related to something: the family, the church, the social group (s) or the larger community. Redemptive suffering is related to others, and it is for others as well as for one's self. God humbled Himself on the cross to save individuals and the world from sin. God suffered Jesus, His only begotten Son, to become our spiritual redemption on the cross. This, my Christian friends, is the spiritual power of the *text*, and our power can become glorious through the reality of the Suffering-Servant-Text.

The power of redemptive suffering is in the power of decision. The exiles accepted the responsibilities involved in their suffering, and the question became: Would others catch the spirit of what they were trying to do?

When we decided to join church; we also decided to accept the responsibilities involved in church membership. Here are the spiritually profound words of James Meredith: "People have asked me if I was terribly afraid the night we went to Oxford. No, my apprehensions came a long time before that. The hardest thing in human nature is to decide to act. I was doing alright in the Air Force. I had to give this up, this established way of things, this status, and try something new and unknown. That's where the big decision was—not here, last month, but there, a couple of years ago. Once I made the decision things just had to happen the way they happened."

The power of redemptive suffering is the impact that we as Christians make on others and our own conscience as a result of our decisions. The exiles made the decision to suffer so they could serve. The power of redemptive suffering is in the power of love. Look at the impact of their decision: "And the will of the Lord prospered in their hands, and they saw the fruit of the trail of their souls and were satisfied." This is the kind of love that God first had for us, because when we were yet sinners, He sacrificed for us. When I initially graduated from college I observed a scene that later struck me as an example of redemptive suffering. Let me share it with you. One of my classmates introduced me to his mother. My classmate had on a new suit, a new shirt, and new shoes. Of course, there is nothing wrong with any of that. But, my classmate's mother, I observed, had on old worn shoes and a neat but well-worn dress. This is a typical scene in many places. This wonderful old lady no doubt had reached the wonderful world of charity (love) through redemptive suffering. The question becomes: Had her son, my classmate, reached that world?

Now, as you move and have your being in this place ask yourself this question? What world have I reached, Lord? Our people have been historically bruised for our sins.

There are three attitudes we can take toward suffering. We can break out, break down, or break through. People will help you to break out, because many individuals like to see others on the run. To be sure, the devil definitely wants to see you on the run rather than take a stand for righteousness sake. Make no mistake about it; there are those who will break you down by breaking your spirit. Of course, many, but not all, will help you to break through. Individuals who embrace the break-out attitude toward suffering are looking for an escape. As long as they are in orbit everything is alright. But the minute they get back to earth, they are ready to go back into space, because escape is their answer to suffering. The moving finger writes and then moves on. This is the view held by the break-out group. They are running from suffering only to meet it down the road. In fact, they take the attitude that there is nothing good or bad under the sun; vanity, vanity; all is vanity. They run from reality by talking these words: "What will be, will be."

Those who hold the break-down attitude cannot accept the internal conflict within themselves nor the warring animalistic elements and the high ideals within themselves. They carry on a civil war within themselves. This can happen to anybody. We have to be honest about our limitations and get away from the notion that all of us are equally, evenly equal in every respect. Of course, in the sight of God, this is true. But, it is only true for us when we work together toward a common goal and live for a common purpose or cause. It is an uphill fight from the break-down to the break-through attitude toward life. Hence, the power of redemptive suffering is at its highest with those who take the break-through attitude. This person takes a realistic view toward life and sees himself or herself as a part of something greater than him or herself. He builds life despite suffering. He has a greater confidence in himself, and he responds wisely to suffering. The way you respond to what happens to you is more important than what happens to you. Your response determines whether or not you will be able to break through.

We are not alone in our struggle to break through. God is with us. The book of Romans tells us that God suffers with us, and we ourselves suffer through the redemptive power of Jesus Christ, and therefore, we share something of the glory of the cross. God is love, and if we believe this, then, we can break through the darkness to the light that comes not through our power, but through God's grace. Here is what Paul says about this matter: "Five times I have received forty lashes less one. Three times I have been beaten with rods; once I was stoned. Three times I besought the Lord about this, that it should leave me; but he said to me my Grace is sufficient for you, for my power is made perfect in weakness."

Paul broke through, and so can you. I know at times it seems as though we have reached the limits of our power of endurance. Lord, I can't bear any more pain and sorrow. This is exactly the way the exiles felt. But, we must face the law of chance head on and move on. When we come to the edge, we need not break-down; we can break-through. We can renew our strength, and mount up with wings like eagles, walk and not faint, break through the darkness to light. I am talking about the light that was shining in the life of Jesus Christ. Redemptive suffering will help to make us into the right stuff, and we will know when this happens, because we will not ask for things to come down, but we will be sending things up. Many people have given us more than we can ever repay. Jesus paid it all; all to Him we owe. Can we not send up to Him thanks and gratitude as our highest form of Christian living? We can share and give ourselves to each other, and then we shall know the power of redemptive suffering. Our Lord and Savior said our "sorrow will turn into joy" and no one will be able to take our joy away. Then we can sing anew my God is able. Yes, he is able, for he has brought us from a mighty long way." Amen!

THE FOUR P'S OF GOD

The Promise

"And this is the promise that he hath promised us, even eternal life" (I John 2:25).

God has promised to never leave us alone. God even suffers with us through our trials and tribulations. If God be for you, then that is more than the world against you. God's promise to His people is salvation. God acts in history for the salvation of humankind. Noah after the great flood was the standard bearer of the promise. God saved four families after the flood; not (8) eight individuals. Family is divine in character. It (family) is God's school for individuals to learn how to love.

I pray that, every Christmas, we remember that Christmas was a family experience, not a department store experience.

The promise that was given to Abraham and Isaac became a down payment on the fulfillment of the promise. Jesus is the promise of our hope in God. The basis of the promise is faith and righteousness.

The Principles of God

Hebrews 5:12: "For when for the time ye ought to be teachers, ye have need that one teach you again which be the first principles of the oracles of God; and are become such as have need of milk, and not of strong meat."

Hebrews 6:1: "Therefore leaving the principles of the doctrine of Christ, let us go on unto perfection; not laying again the foundation of repentance from dead works, and of faith toward God." God's principles are not popular. They hurt the teller/preacher/teacher, as well as the receiver. The truth cuts both ways. It is a two-edged sword.

Hebrew 5:12 is talking about Christian responsibility. By this time you ought to be teachers skilled in the word of righteous and taking responsibility for others who are younger in the Christian faith.

Having a strong moral sensitivity to right and wrong is clear evidence that one understands the principles of God. As a minister of God, you can never go along in order to get along.

The Premises - The Church

Acts 20:28: "Take heed therefore unto yourselves, and to all the flock, over which the Holy Ghost hath made you overseer, to feed the Church of God, which he hath purchased with his own blood."

There is always a temptation to pervert the truth. You feed the church of God with the principles of God. The pastor must feed the flock and rightfully divide the Word of truth at all costs. He must always say, "Thus saith the Lord" lest the blood of the people is on his hands.

The Great Commission was given to the church to go into the world, and in fact, to save the world. For the church to do this, the church must leave the premises and embrace the Great Commission.

"For God so loved the world that He gave his only begotten Son, that whosoever believeth in him should not perish, but have eternal life" (John 3:16). If you are a coward you will never leave the church grounds.

The Patience of God

Luke 8:15: "Those who hear the word (the truth) do so with an honest and good heart and bear fruit with patience."

God is patiently waiting for all of His children to come home. Likewise, a Christian must run the race with patience. "All the days of my life I will wait upon the Lord."

Most of us are in hurry, but going absolutely nowhere.

I will wait until my change comes, and when it comes I will walk and not become weary, run and not faint, mount up with the wings of eagles.

The hidden will be made manifest, that which is secret shall be known, and then face to face, we shall behold God. Amen! Amen! Amen!

CAUGHT UP AND CAN'T COME DOWN

Who was Zacchaeus? The origin of his name is *good*. It means the Just One, the Good One, and the Pure One. Zacchaeus had a good name, but he did evil deeds. The Bible declares: "A good name is rather to be chosen than great riches, and loving favour than silver or gold" (Proverbs 22:1). Zacchaeus was despised by both the Jews and the Gentiles. Zaccheus had heard about the wonder working power of Jesus. One day a line was drawn straight across the life of Zacchaeus. What was rumored became a reality and face-to-face Zaccheus meets Jesus. The whole impact of the Gospel of Good News was in this meeting between Jesus and Zacchaeus, because it redeemed the past of Zacchaeus, transformed his present, and redirected his future.

St. Paul said it best in the seventh chapter of Romans: "A man in Christ is a new creation, a new being."

We know that there is an end and with equal knowledge that man's end is God's beginning. Hence, between light and darkness, life and death, there is salvation for the soul.

Zacchaeus was a man estranged from his heavenly inheritance. He had an earthly material inheritance; he was a wealthy man. But, he was alienated from himself, from others, and from God. Life for Zaccheus had become drudgery. Another day, another dollar was his motto. He had lost contentment, peace of mind, human dignity, and above all, self-respect. The definition of a fool is, loving something that can't love you in return. Your greatest need as a human being is for love, because it is the power of love that created every individual. Thus, that power is God, and God is LOVE. "For God so loved the world, that he gave his only begotten Son, that whosoever believeth in him should not perish, but have everlasting life" (John 3:16).

Zacchaeus loved things. Zacchaeus asked the ultimate question: "WHAT DOES MY LIFE ADD UP TO?" Of course, his answer was *absolutely nothing*. He had things, but things do not spiritually fulfill individuals, and this is why individuals must continue to accumulate things in the fruitless attempt to fulfill his spiritual need.

We know that life comes to a full stop: Except God changes the punctuation mark! Of Bartimaeus, it may have been written that he was blind; of Lazarus, that he was a beggar; of Naaman, that he was a leper. But, with God there need be no periods, only question marks.

Like many others, Zacchaeus had heard about a higher calling that had been given on a hill call Galilee. That higher calling was "blessed are they who do hunger and thirst after righteousness, for they shall be filled." This was a clarion call given by Christ the Righteous One.

A Man in Search of God

The first point is this: Zacchaeus knew that he allowed the devil to get him up a tree. He had been saying, "Lord, Lord" and running with the devil. Instead, of saying, "Lord, Lord" and running from the devil, he was with the devil (24:7). Instead, of allowing God to fight his spiritual battle, he had gotten caught up on the material things of this world, so he finally went in search of God, the Creator and giver of all good gifts. He sought to see who Jesus was! It was bold curiosity that caused Zacchaeus to go in search of Jesus? Or, was it his conscience?

Or, was it a deep hunger that had never been fulfilled?

Zacchaeus wanted to know Jesus by physical sight. He had no idea what was going to happen to him that day. But, he did think that to see Jesus is to know Jesus. You and I cannot see Jesus by physical sight; therefore, we must see Jesus with the spiritual eyes of our mind. We must see Jesus in the face of all individuals and hear Him say: "Inasmuch as you have done it unto the least of them my brethren, you have done it unto me."

But, someone will invariably say, "When did I see thee Lord, hungry, and did not feed thee, naked and did not give thee clothes, in prison and did not visit you, sick and did not pray for you or visit you? Invariably Jesus' answer will be "INASMUCH as you have done it unto the least of them, you have done it unto me" The face of Jesus reminded Zacchaeus of all faces, that is, the faces of the people he had cheated for personal gain.

God in Search of a Man

It is not man's search that is of primary importance, but God's search for every human soul. Only by God's searching could the human soul even begin to search. One of the great church fathers, St. Augustine, wrote, "When first I knew thee thou didst raise me up....and yet I was not fit to see Thee." In this statement lies the unique significance of Jesus in human history: "For the son of man is come to seek and to save that which is lost." Jesus was crucified because He did not represent the kind of God individuals were looking for; therefore they killed Him. Jesus was born on the ground, in a stable, in a manger and no crib for His head, and moreover, wrapped in rags. Now, we all know where you find truth—on the ground, not in high places such as motels, hotels, and Holiday Inn.

The Man Who Invites God In

The third point is: The man who invites God to enter into his life as a worthy guest; God will come in and sup with him. Therefore, between man's searching and God's searching there is salvation for the soul.

Now, let's get to the heart of the story. Zacchaeus was a short man, and because of the press of the crowd Zacchaeus couldn't see Jesus. So he ran down the road and climbed up into a sycamore tree to get a clearer view of Jesus. Now think with me for a spiritual moment.

The sycamore tree had a double meaning; it was a symbolic paradox. Zacchaeus's life was caught up in materialistic possessions. He was spiritually treed. He was out on a limb and the devil was about to chop his tree down. Zacchaeus had built a tree house, not a spiritual house on a solid foundation, the truth of God.

But, thanks be to God, Jesus is on the road every day, seeking to save that which is lost. He will stop by your house and knock on your front door. Will you allow Him to enter your spiritual house as an honored guest? Zacchaeus's desire was to have a clear view at what was at the center of life. He wanted another look, a different perspective about life. God is always courteous and does not invade the privacy of the human soul.

When Jesus wanted some disciples, He did not say, "Come and follow me and you will get something for nothing." Or, "Look, I have this to give you." Jesus only made spiritual promises. He always talked about the spiritual work to be done. When Zacchaeus met Jesus it made all the difference in the world. When Jesus came to the place, He looked up and He saw Zacchaeus, and Jesus said: "Zacchaeus make haste, come on down, for today I will abide at your house." Jesus was saying, today, I am going to lift your burden. I am going to lighten your load, because what you have been packing is too heavy to take to the grave or to God's throne of Judgment. The mind (invisible-church) is its own spiritual place, and in and of, itself can make a Heaven a Hell or a Hell a Heaven. This is why the Bible states: "Let the mind that was in Christ Jesus be also in you." To every man and nation comes the moment of decision simply, because man's search for God, and God's search for man is salvation for the soul.

Jesus was saying to Zacchaeus, "What did you see that made you desire this peace?" And, Zacchaeus answered, 'I saw mirrored in your face the Zacchaeus that God meant for me to be! Jesus said to Zacchaeus: 'I am come that you might have life and life more abundantly. I came into the world for this cause: to save the lost.' It was not the purpose of Jesus to be ministered unto or to destroy. Jesus wanted to fulfill the will of God. In fact, Jesus was born so that the truth of God might have someone to bear witness to it.

Make no mistake about it; Jesus is on the road today. In His left hand, He has the promise of God: I will never leave you alone, nor will I ever forsake you. In His right hand, He has the power of God for salvation for your soul. If you are spiritually lost, and if you, too, are like Zacchaeus, spiritually treed, caught up and want to get down out of your tree-house, you can, today, begin to live where Jesus lived and die where Jesus died: In the will of God." If you have spiritually lost your way and you want your burden lifted and your sinful load lightened, then come to Jesus. Come to Jesus. Come just as you are, and He will wash you white as snow.

FISHERS OF MEN

Scripture: Matthew 4:18-20

"Walking by the Sea of Galilee, Jesus saw two brothers, Simon who was called Peter, and Andrew his brother, casting a net in the sea; for they were Fishermen. And He said to them, Come follow me, and I will make you fishers of men. And, they immediately left the nets and followed Jesus."

These are difficult times in which we live. American society is spiritually upside-down. A lot of individuals are caught between their forward drive and their backward pull. This is the age of spiritual-moral confusion: Secular-Relativism. American culture is in moral decline because too many individuals have robbed themselves of moral values and spiritual principles, and consequently, the moral walls have been torn down. In fact, too many individuals are trying to find a right way to do wrong. We live in a culture that has relativized right and wrong. We take right and make it wrong and make it work for a while. We take wrong and make it right and make it work for a while. And, all of this moral confusion is charged to our children.

For Jesus, community is the unquestioned presupposition of life. This is why Jesus issued a call for individuals to come out of Individualism, and form a human community under the sovereignty of God. Jesus had recently been baptized in the Jordan River, and for forty days and nights He prayed and fasted in the wilderness. Immediately, after this experience, Jesus began His ministry with a call to "come follow me, and I will make you fishers of men."

Those who followed Jesus formed the Christian community, the church. Jesus was calling individuals to remake their lives. Hence, note who Jesus called. He did not call the smartest and the so-called best of men; those He called had no wealth, influence, or high social standing in society. He called ordinary working-class men. This call was revolutionary. Men denied themselves, repented of their sins, and followed Jesus. In speaking to them, Jesus spoke beyond them to all men who would listen.

Today, in the black community, 80% of the homes have no men/fathers which in turn, translates into most men not being involved in church life. For after all, the church begins in the home.

The first element in the call was for one to deny self because self is the enemy. Anytime you want to see your enemy, look in the mirror. You must be willing to forsake mother, father, sister, and brother for the sake of the Kingdom of God. The call was about total commitment, a willingness to spend your life in service to God.

The second element in the call was for an individual to take up his cross. Here, Jesus indicates that every individual has a cross to bear and a burden to carry. No individual can die for another individual. So it is true that no individual can carry another individual's cross. "Must Jesus bear the Cross alone and the whole world goes free? No there is a cross for everyone." Each individual is responsible for his or her own life/living under the reality of God because after death comes judgment (Hebrews 9:27). Jesus had to remind the disciples that to carry your cross is the meaning of the call. It's not just one day, but every day. Even the disciples started arguing about power, money, and privilege. Lord, when we get to the Kingdom who is going to sit on the right hand and who is going to sit on the left hand. Jesus answered by saying: "Shut up. If you want to be great you must be willing to serve." Anytime God uses the words "but" or "if something important is about to follow. What if a man gains the whole world and loses his soul? Life does not consist in the abundance of things which a man possesses. Life is found in family, friends, and service to others, which in turn is our rightful service to God.

To become fishers of men, an individual must possess these qualities:

PATIENCE. An individual must know how to wait upon the Lord. You cannot be restless and quick. Rarely do you witness quick results in teaching and preaching because only the power of God can save a soul. There is the story of the preacher who preached twenty-five years who was not saved. One Sunday God knocked him out in the pulpit.

PERSEVERANCE. A good fisherman must never become discouraged because the battle is the Lord's. You must always be willing to try, try, try, and try again. When nothing seems to happen you must try again.

COURAGE. You must be willing to face all kinds of dangers. There is always a danger in telling individuals the Truth. When you tell the Truth you take your life in your hands because the world hates the Truth. Moreover, the spirit of the devil is going to and fro; hence, you will not find the Truth in a crowd. But you will find it on the ground, in a stable, in a manager. You will not find Truth at the Holiday Inn, because there will always be no room at the Inn for the Truth.

To be a good fisher of men, you must have an eye for the right moment. There are times when it is hopeless to fish. You must know when to cast and when not to cast. You must choose your moment wisely. There are times when people will welcome the Truth. And, there are times when, even though the Truth will move them, they will resent the Truth. There are even times when the truth will harden their hearts. There is a time to speak and a time to be silent. In other words, you must fit the bait to the fish. We must know that we are going to win some and we are going to lose some.

St. Paul says, "I became all things to all men so that by chance I might win a few." We must present individuals with the truth at all costs. For what was the life of Jesus other than a journey with the Truth? We must hitch our wagons to a star, and that star must lead us to the cross (Mt. Calvary). It was on the cross that Truth was crushed to the ground, but the Truth rose even more victorious. "Come, follow me, and I will make you fishers of men." This is our call because every Christian is called to be a minister of the Gospel of Good News. He must be willing to serve rather than be served. He must be willing to console rather than seek consolation. He must be willing to minister to those in need in the name of truth.

Come follow Me and I will show you the path of life wherein peace, love, and joy abide. Amen!

IF A MAN IS DETERMINED TO BE A GODLY FATHER, WHO CAN STOP HIM!

Scripture: 1 Corinthians 6:19

"What? Know ye not that your body is the temple of the Holy Ghost which is in you, which ye have of God, and ye are not your own? For ye are bought with a price: therefore glorify God in your body, and in your spirit, which are God's." Do not become enslaved by your own vanity desires because when you become a Christian the Holy Spirit comes to live in your body. As a Christian, you are free to be all that you can be for God, but you are not free from God. But, most of all you cannot satisfy vanity, because vanity is of the devil (satisfying the flesh)."

Luke 12:15 says: "And he said unto them, Take heed, and beware of covetousness: for man's life consisteth not in the abundance of the things which he possesseth." A godly man does not deal in hypocrisy. The good life is not about being materially wealthy; therefore, beware of covetousness that is a greedy desire for what you do not have. The good life is about living in relationship with God, and doing God's will and God's work.

Titus 2:1-8 says: "But speak thou the things which become sound doctrine: that the aged men be sober, grave, temperate, and sound in faith, in clarity, in patience." This Scripture is about right living in church houses because the best teacher is example. A godly father must be spiritually grounded in the truth of Holy Scriptures so as not to be swayed by the oratory of false teachers and false teachings. "Men build churches; Women, children, and the elderly attend churches."

Isaiah 24:1-5 says: "Behold, the Lord maketh the earth empty, and make it waste, and turneth it upside down, and scattereth abroad the inhabitants thereof. And it shall be, as with the people, so with the priest; as with the servant, so with his master; as with the maid, so with her mistress, as with the buyer, so with the seller; as with the lender, so with the borrower; as with the taker of usury, so with the giver of usury to him. The land shall be utterly emptied, and utterly spoiled; for the Lord hath spoken this word. The earth mourned and faded away, the world languisheth, the haughty people of the earth do languish. The earth also is defiled under the inhabitants thereof; because they have transgressed the laws, changed the ordinance, broken the everlasting covenant."

The reason I am sharing different Scriptures with you is because I don't want you to trust me (Bobby E. Mills), but trust God's Word. That is, I want you to believe the spiritual truth of the Bible, because I do not have a Heaven or Heaven for your soul." Once you put your hands on the plough don't look back! Therefore, without a Biblical foundation with spiritual understanding, what you have is religion without spiritual substance (spirituality)—properly described as religion without saving grace or religion without a real pathway to God (heaven). Here is what God says about being a man because every male must understand what it means to be a godly man before attempting to become a father: "And the Lord God said, It is not good that the man be alone; I will make him an help meet for him" (Genesis 2:18). Here's the spiritual reason God said that it is not good for a man to be alone: "Whoso findeth a wife findeth a good thing, and obtaineth the favor of the Lord" (Proverbs 18:22). Again, God is the designer of family, not the U.S. Supreme Court. Moreover, family is about spiritual things (God), and the love of God that was in Jesus Christ reconciling the world.

God has family and family relationships on His mind. Again, God is the designer of family, and not the U.S. Supreme Court or morally confused politicians. Therefore, as an American citizen, if you believe that same-sex marriage is okay, then you have malnutrition of the brain and not even psychiatric counseling can help you; after all, human life does not have its origin in same-sex activity.

The Biblical four-fold foundation is about family (godliness) (Genesis 1:26-28): "And God said, Let us make man in our own image, after our own likeness: and let them have dominion over the fish of the sea, and over the fowl of the air, and over the cattle, and over all the earth, and over every creeping thing that creepeth upon the earth. So God created man in his own image, in the image of God created he him; male and female created he them. And God blessed them, and God said unto them, Be fruitful, and multiply, and replenish the earth, and subdue it: and have dominion over the fish of the sea, and over the fowl of the air, and over every living thing that moveth upon the earth." Please tell me how you get same-sex marriage out of this Scripture. John 8:44 puts it this way: "Ye are of your father the devil, and the lusts of your father ye will do. He was a murderer from the beginning, and abode not in truth, because there is no truth in him. When he speaketh a lie, he speaketh of his own; for he is a liar, and the father of it."

(1) The devil's first line of attack is on the family. Why? Because family is designed by God and family is the foundation of God's salvation plan (Heaven on earth). This is why Joshua could boldly say, "As for me and my house, we will serve the Lord." If the devil can get you to deal with your family as an economic institution rather than as a love association, then he has a stronghold with you and yours. Hence, your family is now caught up in dealing with things that is in love with things rather than loving each other. Of course, this is why Joshua could say: "Now therefore fear the Lord and serve him in sincerity and in truth, and put away the gods which your fathers served; but as for me and my house, we will serve the LORD" (Joshua 24:14-15). Salvation comes through the generation. This is why the lineage of Jesus goes back to Seth the generation that called upon the Lord.

(2) Faith. The devil, secondly, attacks your faith. The devil wants you to believe that faith is abstract foolishness. But, faith is real. Believe me; you have faith in the civil construction engineers who constructed your church, because you did not physically see the construction of the facility. When you leave the church and go to your car you will have faith in the engineers who build the Mercedes that you drive, but you may not know how to say LORD have mercy upon me, because you believe that your car will not blow up when you start it up!

(3) Future. The devil wants to keep you from getting to your future, because the future belongs to God. God wants all individuals to know and understand the plans that He has for our lives.

These are difficult times in which we live, because we live in an age of spiritual and moral confusion. Again, the spiritual-moral walls have been torn down, and without divine intervention they probably cannot be rebuilt. Therefore, too many individuals are taking wrong and making it right, and vice-versa, and making it work for a little while.

Unfortunately, when you are speaking to a male in the twenty-first century, you do not know whether you are speaking to a man, a homosexual or a transgender individual. Of course, if you do not know who you are talking to or interacting with, then you have no clue as to how to deal with them; therefore, spiritually healthy relationships become impossible. Life is about Relationships, because God desires to have a personal relationship with every individual, and above all, He desires to be in fellowship with every individual.

Allow me to quickly explain why you cannot satisfy vanity. First of all, vanity is of the flesh (pleasure principle and love of things). Proverbs 12:11 says, "He that followeth vain persons is void of understanding." Proverbs 22:8 says, "He that soweth iniquity shall reap vanity." Ecclesiastes 1:2 says, "Vanity of vanities, saith the preacher, vanity of vanities: all is vanity. King Solomon said it best: The devil deals in things; therefore his desire is to get individuals to deal in things. The devil tried to get Jesus to deal in things. For example: He tried to get Jesus to turn stones into bread. Behold the mess we find ourselves in. America has a president in The White House who truly believes that money solves all things, and therefore, the devil is on the spiritual attack in American society because "The love of money is the root of all evil" (1 Timothy 6:10). The devil attacks the family, faith, as well as the future by attempting to get individuals to live in the past.

You cannot judge a book by its cover; likewise, you cannot always judge an individual by the way he looks. For example: Don King's interview with Sam Donaldson (ABC NEWS). Sam Donaldson was interviewing Don King and observed that Don King had on expense jewelry. Donaldson said: "Mr. King, they say you are an extremely wealthy man. How much money do you have?" Mr. King replied: "Mr. Donaldson, you never ask a man how much money he has, because if a man can tell you how much money he has, he does not have money." Mr. King further replied: "I do not know how much money I have, because I am too busy making money to count money. I have accountants who count money, especially the money that goes out!"

Need I remind everyone: Money is a cruel master! I am reminded of a personal story I recall, "The Story of Willie Brannon." Willie Brannon was a small businessman and the chairman of the Deacon Board of a Baptist church. We were having lunch on one occasion and his pastor called; he wanted to borrow two hundred dollars. Willie told him to meet us at Luby's cafeteria and have lunch and pick up the money. Shortly thereafter, his pastor showed up, we fellowshipped, and when we were ready to leave Willie went in his right pocket, pulled out a roll of one-hundred-dollar bills and gave his pastor $200.00. Then he told his pastor that he did not want to see him broke, so he went into his left pocket pulled out a roll of one-hundred-dollar bills and pealed out three hundred dollars and gave them to his pastor as a gift. His pastor said thanks and walked away smiling with five hundred dollars. Willie then asked me did I understand what we just witnessed: A pastoral leader asking to borrow two hundred dollars and receiving what he asked for as well as an additional gift of three hundred dollars. Willie then stated that a spiritual man would have paid me back the two hundred dollars he borrowed out of the three hundred dollar gift. This is an indicator that he had no intentions on repaying the money, because if a man will not pay you back out of a gift, he will certainly not pay you back out of his own labor: "Money is a Cruel Master." Money is just a tool and individuals can use it as a tool or as a fool. God's love for us is greater than all the money in the world as it is or shall be in the future. Amen!

WHAT DO YOU DO WHEN IT IS MIDNIGHT?

Scripture: Acts 16:22-26

What do you do when you are in a bad situation? What do you do when you create a spiritual prison for yourself? What do you do when you are unjustly thrown in a physical prison? What do you do when you are in Egypt and your back is against the wall? Paul and Silas had the answer.

Paul and Silas had been persecuted and they were in jail awaiting prosecution. They had their clothing torn off of them. They were beaten and thrown in jail because they were servants of the Most High God. Therefore, whether your prison is spiritual or physical, Paul and Silas give us a road map for what to do.

First of all, pray. No prayer, no power. Plenty prayer, plenty power. Prayer changes things. Prayer changes both the individual as well as the circumstances. Prayer is internal self-introspection. Prayer is about positive self-talk. Prayer keeps Hope alive. This is why the Bible says when you pray go into your closet and pray to your Father in secret and He will reward you openly. Prayer is about bringing the "I" that is in us under submission to the "me" that's in each of us. The "I" in us is the "I" that is in the middle of SIN (Personal Pronoun Disease). "I" is our super-ego. EGO is an acronym for Edge God Out. The me that is in us each of us is the spiritual part of every individual that cries out to God: LORD, HAVE MERCY ON ME.

Second, Praise God from whom all blessings flow, because when praises go up blessings abound. Our dedication to praise produces an expectation. The earth is the Lord's and the fullness thereof, and all that dwell therein. In Psalm 89, David says, "I will sing of the loving kindness of the Lord forever... and to all generations I will make known thy faithfulness with my mouth...and the Heavens will praise thy wonders Lord." Even in jail, Paul and Silas could praise God for His ever loving kindness. Daniel could praise God in the lion's den. The Hebrew boys could praise God in the fiery furnace.

Third, you patiently wait upon the Lord. For the battle is the Lord's. First Samuel 17:47 says, "All the earth should know that there is a God in Israel, and that all this assembly may know that the Lord does not deliver by sword or spear; for the battle is the Lord's, and He will deliver you into His Hands." "Not by might nor by power but by my Spirit says the Lord" (Zechariah 4:6). They that wait upon the Lord shall renew their strength for the battle is not given to the swift, but to the one that can endure to the end. The praying, praising, and patience of Paul and Silas caused God to show up and show out. God produced a Jail House Rock of such a magnitude that even Elvis Presley had to declare "I am all shook up."

So when we pray, praise, and patiently wait upon God, because the power of God will manifest itself, even those who persecute you and come to eat up your flesh will ask for forgiveness, and God will forgive their sins and wash them white as snow. The jailer feared that all the prisoners had escaped and that the authorities would behead him, so he was about to kill himself. But Paul cried out in a loud voice, "Do yourself no harm; we are all here." The jailer called for lights and rushed in trembling with fear. He fell down before Paul and Silas and said, "Sirs, what must I do to be saved?" They declared, "Believe in the Lord Jesus Christ, and you shall be saved, you and your household." This affirmation was true two thousand years ago and it is still true today. The spiritual power of prayer changes both the internal as well as the external conditions. Amen!

WHAT IS RELIGION DOING TO YOUR CHARACTER?

Scripture: 1 Samuel 24:16-19

"Thou art more righteous than I am for thou have rewarded me with good, whereas I have rewarded thee with evil."

Sometimes persons who make no confession of religious faith often achieve better character than those who do. Someone once said that what is wrong with the Christian church is that those who sit in the pews Sunday after Sunday need to be converted. This is a disturbing fact of life.

In the Book of Samuel there are two versions of the episode of war between King Saul and David. Saul was the anointed King of Israel, the divinely appointed leader of the Nation of Israel. He was supposed to be the champion of religion. David was considered an outlaw and his followers were considered guerilla fighters. Of course, we know that David was a profoundly religious man, but he was not always good in his moral conduct, even when we judge him by the standards of his day. Yet, we find in this passage of Scripture that his moral character was nobler and more winsome than that of the chief official of religion.

The Bible says that David was "a man after God's own heart." The Bible does not attribute this character trait to any other individual whose life is recorded in Scriptures. Saul had been hunting David to kill him. David had lived for months as a fugitive, and he felt that there was one step between him and death. David had suffered from the warranted persecution of Saul, and David could have killed Saul anytime he wanted to. Remember, David lived in an age where an eye for an eye and a tooth for a tooth was the law of the land. But David rose above this religious code of ethics to accept a higher morality. David said, "The Lord forbid that I should kill Saul." To David, God is the source of morality, not human convenience.

This is why individuals should shun evil, learn to do well, seek God's judgment, relieve the oppressed, help the fatherless, and plead for the widows.

Jesus lifted up the concept of man, and now we have a new image to live up to. You cannot teach character like you teach math. Character must be taught or inspired by example. It is not a question of knowing what is right, but of having the moral courage to do what is right. What does the Lord require of thee? David held back the hand of vengeance. Can you? Vengeance is mine saith the Lord. Yes, when Saul meets David, and he sees himself face to face, and he goes to pieces. Saul was redeemed in his moral failure, because he saw himself for what he was. He saw his strengths, and he saw his weaknesses. Hence, moral failure need not be a disgrace if an individual faces it with honesty and without illusions.

I want to give you three reasons religion sometimes fails to develop high moral characters:

1. Too often religion is only associated with church attendance. Church attendance is important, but religious-spiritual understanding is more important.

2. The structure of the worship experience itself where preaching is viewed as the only form of worship.

3. Individuals do not meet God in partnership. Therefore, we become lost to God and alive to greed, selfishness, idolatry and we end up attempting to play God.

What kind of church do you want? Is a universal question. Of course, there are some individuals who do not want any kind of church. Jesus is coming back for a church without a wrinkle or spot. Be assured that it is not the visible institutional churches on some street corners. Do you want a church where love works miracles? Do you want a church where high religion develops high moral characters? If you do, then it begins in the heart of your own mind. God bless you and yours in Jesus' name. Amen and thank God!

THE ART OF FORGETTING

Scripture: Genesis 41:51

"And Joseph called the name of his firstborn Manasseh: For God he said, have made me forget all of my toil, and all my father's house."

All Christians know the story of Joseph. Joseph was dealt a raw deal by his own brothers; that is, he was given a bad hand: "But God." For after all, God can change the script and this is why Joseph could say: "God made me forget all my toil." Throughout the New Testament the theme of forgetting is an important spiritual element in Christian discipleship. When Jesus walked along the shores of the Galilee He issued His famous edit: "Come follow me and I will make you fishers of men'.

One man replied, "Lord, I want to follow you, but my father has just died, therefore permit me to go back home and bury him." Jesus answered the man by saying, "Let the dead bury the dead." In other words, there are a lot of people who are lifetime members of the walking dead club and one of them will bury your dead father.

Here are the words of another man: "Lord, I want to follow You, but permit me to go back home and say good-bye to my loved ones." Jesus answers by saying, "He who would follow after Me must forsake all: father, mother, brother and sister." The urgency of the Kingdom of God is greater than family ties.

Another man had started on his way, but he began to long for his home, family, and friends. He wanted to turn back. Jesus says, "He who puts his hands to the plough and looks back is not fit for the Kingdom of God." Life is not about looking back. Life is about looking ahead, looking to the hills from whence cometh our help, our help comes from the Lord. Thus, in these three illustrations we see Jesus saying to those who would be His followers; you must learn what things to forget and what things to remember.

Memory has a significant value. Even unhappy memories have value. We berate ourselves, because we do not have good memories. If only I could remember, we say. What to remember and how to remember are really the questions we are faced with, daily. There is another side to memory. Nations, as well as, individuals had better learn how to forget not just the horrors of war, but how to study war no more. Races and ethnic groups need to learn how to forget blind prejudices.

The greater half of the secret of remembering well is the art of forgetting. Day by day some of God's uplifting ministries remain unremembered, because our minds are weak, and our hearts are caught up in brooding. God's love falls among us and is choked to death. We have memories in abundance, but how many of them are things that we should have forgotten long ago. If our memories are merely pathetic and not prophetic, if our memories have no window to the sunrise, if our memories have no wings of hope, if our memories have no redemptive power, then they should be drowned in the sea of forgetfulness. Joseph learned how to forget and how to forgive. You cannot forgive without forgetting. You know the old saying: I forgive you, but I won't forget.

The question is: how much have I to forget? Joseph called his firstborn son Manasseh, "for God, said he, hath made me forget all my toil, and all my father's house." (Genesis 41: 51). Joseph could not have achieved the art of forgetting without self-discipline. Joseph felt that God had given him great blessings. These blessings had struck deep in the heart of his mind, and not a scar of what was rough and tough in his life remained in his mind.

Revenge, remorse, and greed are three nails, any one of which can drive a memory so deep into our lives until only the grace of God can pluck it out of our minds. Scores of men and women are unhappy, because they have never broken away from their past. The Gospel of Jesus Christ can teach us the art of forgetting because in the grace of God there are rivers that can transform our memories, discipline our minds, and above all, renew our minds.

Joseph says that God made him forget all of his toils. Believe me, Joseph had many things to forget, but God, made him forget his own failures. All of us know failure in some form or another. In failure, there is an element of humility. We cannot evade responsibility for the blunders we make, and we cannot always lay our blunders on our own stupidity. Sometimes factors beyond our control come into play in terms of why bad things happen to us. Joseph didn't really do anything to deserve what he received at the hands of his own brothers, but he could forget his toils, because he realized that he had been blessed in more ways than he could count.

God's love made Joseph forget the treachery of his own brothers. Joseph had a lot of reasons to become cynical about human virtue. His own brothers had betrayed him, but he learned to purge himself of memories of unkindness. Joseph developed width and breadth of character in his life. He was not small; his life was large enough to include pain and suffering. All of us have been the victims of unkindness.

Friends and relatives have exploited all of us. The question is, how did we deal with the situation?

When we nurse our memories of unfairness and unkindness, we become small and narrow, and in the end we only harm ourselves. There is only one way to master the art of forgetting and that is through facing reality. That is what the Jesus way is all about: facing reality. Face the pain, face the person, and then deliberately forgive. Move on. Travel the King's Highway.

And be kind one to the other, tenderhearted, forgiving one another, even as God has forgiven us. Do you think that it is easy? If you do, then you do not know what forgiveness costs. Love forgiving, love trusting is the only thing that never fails, because love always claims its own.

You may say that it is impossible to forgive this person. Jesus says that forgiving is forgetting. I beseech you, brothers and sisters in Christ, to enroll in the Master's school of forgiveness. The art of forgetting is not learned in a day, because it requires that we forget self. Self is the enemy. And, this is why every soul that can love ought to love.

The real question is: How do we live? And what are we willing to sacrifice to live the way we say we want to live? At the end of the day, life is about self-discipline and self-discipline is a spiritual value. Amen!

CHRISTIAN LOVE

Scripture: Matthew 5:43-48

In this passage of Scripture, Jesus gives the new Law of Love. Jesus gives a startling demand: Love your enemies. In the days of Jesus, it was common for one to have hatred toward one's enemies and love towards only one's neighbors. The people in the Old Testament had built a fence around the word 'neighbor.'

Not only were enemies hated, but also it was a part of their true religion. This is why the story of the Good Samaritan in the days of Jesus was viewed as mere folly. Jesus comes along and begins to teach that there is no fence around the concept of neighbor. Good fences do not necessarily make for good neighbors, as the Farmer in Frost's poem "Mending Wall" thought. Jesus insisted that even the person who curses us is our neighbor; therefore, the concept of neighbor is as wide as humankind itself.

However, Jesus made this one thing clear: We are not demanded to love our enemies in the same manner that we love our nearest and dearest. Jesus knew that this was not possible or right. Loving your enemies is a different kind of love. We cannot help loving our dearest, or those things which are lovely, pleasant or loveable, because this kind of love is something that is unsought. It is born of the emotions of the heart. But in the case of our enemies, love is something of the will rather than the heart. We must will to love our enemies. Loving our enemies is a victory, a conquest over the natural instincts of human nature, which is to hate our enemies and violently oppose our foes. I do not need to tell you that all people are not loveable, and therefore, you cannot love all people from the heart. But, as Christians, we must will to love our enemies. This is why there is a big difference between religion and God. Of course, everybody who says, "Lord, Lord," does not mean it, and everything that is done in the name of God is not necessarily sanctioned by God.

Therefore, Christian love is both an attitude of the heart and mind whereby we can achieve unconquerable goodwill towards those who seek to destroy us. Christian love is the power to love those who we do not like and who do not like us.

To be sure, you cannot have this kind of love apart from God. Jesus laid down this kind of love as the basis for personal relationships in our families, with our neighbors, and with those who we meet in everyday living. This commandment demands that we should say first and foremost: "This means me." This is what God demands of ME, and it is only through God's grace that we can have this kind of love. It is only God who can command that bitterness die and love spring to life.

God also demands that we should pray for our enemies. Why? No person can pray for another person and still hate that person. When a person takes himself or herself and the individual they are tempted to hate to God something happens to the person on the inside. No person can go on hating in the presence of God. Why? God is love, and hate dissolves when it is in the presence of love. Jesus demands that we should have this kind of love; that is, the kind of love that makes us Godlike.

The new Law of Love is not simply an ethic. Jesus demands that we act in goodwill from God toward those who we like as well as those whom we do not like. Therefore, to love one's enemies is the supreme test of one's religious character.

The life of Jesus points to God's action in the world that is God's unconquerable love. "For God so loved the world, that He gave his only begotten Son, that whosoever believeth in him should not perish, but have everlasting life. For God sent not his Son into the world to condemn the world, but that the world through him might be saved." (John 3: 16-17).

The Bible tells us that God gives us an example of His love. It tells us that we received in nature and in Jesus a love that we did not deserve, and we must act in love the same way toward all people. God makes His sun to rise on both the good and the evil; He sends the rain on the just as well as on the unjust. God gives His love to saints and sinners alike. It is God who gives us the power to receive the new love, the new Kingdom, and the new life.

The Psalmist puts it this way: "The eyes of all wait upon thee, and thou give them their meat in due season." In God, there is universal love towards those who have broken His law, and who have broken His heart.

When we have the kind of love that God has for us, we become sons and daughters of God. This is what it means to be Godlike. God demands that we should be perfect in love. A thing is perfect when it fully realizes the purpose(s) for which it was created.

For what purpose were we created? The Bible leaves us with no doubt. We were created to be like God, and no matter what we do, God seeks our highest good.

One hymn writer puts it this way: "Thy foes might hate, despise, revile, thy friends unfaithful prove, unwearied in forgiveness still, thy heart could only love."

When we have this unconquerable, unwearied, sacrificial love, we become Godlike. The person who cares the most for others is the most perfect. We can only realize our true personhood by becoming Godlike. What makes us Godlike is the kind of love that never stops caring for people, no matter what they do.

When this happens, we become more human, and we enter into Christian perfection, whereby we can forgive as God forgives and love as God loves. God loves you, and so do I.

MY GOD IS SO HIGH YOU CAN'T GET OVER HIM

Scripture: Psalm 139:1-10

I ask you to consider the central fact of our faith: God. There are many people who feel that a man's philosophy does not matter. There are others who feel that the most important thing about a man is his philosophy, that is, his view of the world. Thus, the Bible tells us what we think about God determines what we think about ourselves as well as others, but more importantly, what we think about the meaning of life, duty, responsibility, and destiny. This is why the focal point for Jesus was His obedience to God, which in turn, becomes His obedience to loving and serving His fellow man.

There are few of us who actually disbelieve in God. Atheists are nearly always people in revolt against some unworthy thought(s) about God.

John Wesley once said many alleged unbelievers are saying "your God is my devil." No, few of us are without some belief in God however vague and fleeting it might be. The hustle of daily life may shut our thoughts off from God, but sooner or later something happens, and we say, "Lord, have mercy on us." We see the world and we say the world is morally bankrupt.

Adversity opens our eyes to the hard cold realities of life.

God gives individuals free will; that is, we can choose to be righteous or we can choose to be unrighteous.

God does not save the unrighteous. He saves the righteous, that is, those who repent of their sins and choose to become faithful and obedient to Him. (A perfect example is Noah and the Ark.)

Therefore, we need personal faith in ourselves as well as others, for it is this kind of collective faith that gives us the courage to believe it is possible for God's Kingdom to exist on earth and His will be done, in time and space as clearly expressed in the Lord's Prayer.

This was the spiritual yearning of Jesus expressed in the Lord's Prayer. For when mankind collectively does God's will, we have Heaven on earth as decreed in the Lord's Prayer.

Some of us believe in one God, who is the Father of us

all, who is above all, and who is in us all. God is in everything and touched by nothing. We believe in a God who enters into history, who makes history, and who is moving history towards a more, brotherly and humane level of existence.

We have spiritually sound reasons for this faith, because God sent to us the way, the truth, and the light. But, more importantly, the human example: The life of Jesus the Righteous One, and "The Jesus Way."

This truth is not only about life after death, but about human community on earth, as well. This truth is not about individualism, but community. This truth is not about vulgar capitalism, but collectivism that is generous sharing. This truth is expressed most adequately in the Hebraic Tradition as well as the Christian tradition, but it has been distorted by those who desire to exploit others; that is, get something for nothing. It is in the life and teaching on Jesus that we find an active God who is alert, a God who is a living God and whose purposes will come to pass. God is much bigger than racism, classism, or sexism.

Thus, in the life of Jesus, God sought to find those who were lost and spiritually ignorant (non-spiritually thinking). I desire to tell you about the inescapable presence of God, that primal invisible energy that makes for love and righteousness. Hence, God is a given, not an axiom that must be empirically proven. Moreover, without faith it is impossible to please God. This is why Job cried, "Oh that I knew where I might find Him." And, on the other hand, the psalmist celebrates the inescapable presence of God through a poem. Psalm 139:1-10:

> *O Lord, thou hast searched me, and known me.*
>
> *Thou knowest my downsitting and mine uprising, thou understandest my thought afar off.*
>
> *Thou compassest my path and my lying down, and art acquainted with all my ways.*
>
> *For there is not a word in my tongue, but, lo, O Lord, thou knowest it altogether.*
>
> *Thou hast beset me behind and before, and laid thine hand upon me.*
>
> *Such knowledge is too wonderful for me; it is high, I cannot attain unto it.*
>
> *Whither shall I go from they spirit? Or whither shall I flee from thy presence?*
>
> *If I ascend up into heaven, thou art there: if I make my bed in hell, behold, thou art there.*

If I take the wings of the morning, and dwell in the

uttermost parts of the sea.

Even there shall thy hand lead me, and thy right hand

shall hold me.

One clearly sees why this psalm is cherished by athletes of the Spirit.

Surely, it is because truth is not just proven by logic, but by life itself. The soul that seeks to escape God, always finds it impossible, because God is universal truth. And, the truth will always stand even if mankind seeks to destroy life. There is an ole Negro Spiritual that expresses this thought to the utmost:

"My God is so high you can't get over Him. He's so low until you can't get under Him. He's so wide until you can't go around Him. You must come in through the door."

Yes, the inescapable presence of God. This kind of faith only comes from a certain attitude toward life. Faith is man's guide, but not blind faith. Of course, not just faith in God, but faith in one's own human spiritual resources as well as in one's fellow man.

"The Soul is restless until it finds rest in God."

Proverbs 20:13-14: "Love not sleep, lest thou come to poverty, open thine eyes, and then ye shalt be satisfied."

Proverbs 6:6: "Go to the ant, thou sluggard, consider her ways and be wise."

Proverbs 10:4-5: "He becometh poor that dealeth with a slack hand: but the hand of the diligent maketh rich."

Proverbs 10:14: "Wise men lay up knowledge: but the mouth of the foolish is near destruction."

Too many Americans have been spiritually unproductive far too long. Hence, Proverbs 26 is an entire chapter about foolishness. We must learn to put first things first, because the mind is the most precious and important possession an individual has as a defense against the wiles of the devil. Why give it away to the vanity of the world? Religion must not become a projection of our own hopes and our fears; therefore, the source of our Christian faith (religion) must be God's promises. God is so high it is important that every individual know that he/she must come through the door of personal salvation.

God is high in the ethical demands He places upon human existence; thus, a vital and genuine faith in God compels every individual to seek Godlike virtues in their personal and social life.

We live in a generation which ought to realize that you can't defy a God whose essential nature is justice, mercy, truth, love, and spiritual beauty.

The truth of God became the Gospel of God in Jesus Christ reconciling the world unto Him. We must have God's principles within us, and God will have us with Him in the bye and bye. Then, and only then, can we say that "GOD IS LOVE." Therefore, I am pleading with you as well as praying with you that you have a vital faith and a practical Christian religion. Christianity is a pure religion that is about daily living, not just a Sunday experience.

For God is not a problem to be solved, but a spiritual force to be joined on the battle field of life for justice, love, mercy, and righteousness.

We try other roads; we travel other paths, until a sign compels us to get back on the King's Highway. It is not by seeking that we find God, but in living that we are found by Him. For wherever life is more humane, more just, more loving, there God is. Job made the mistake of looking for God, rather than creatively living life in God. Individuals make the mistake of drinking and not thinking about how do I live and what I am willing to give up (sacrifice) to live the way I say I want to live. Of course, that process leads to dying, rather than living. God never forsakes the righteous, but He will abandon the unrighteous to their unrighteousness, which in turn, leads to self-destruction because "it is appointed unto men once to die, but after this the judgment" (Hebrews 9:27). Amen and Amen!

THE PRIORITY OF PRAYER

Scripture: Matthew 6:8-13

Prayer is not a new thing to the human race. It early became apparent to righteously disposed men that many problems arose in their lives that they couldn't solve of their own efforts. "O God," confessed Jeremiah, "I know that the way of man is not in himself; it is not in man that walketh to direct his steps."

When David was hemmed in by his enemies, who sought to kill him, he cried: "Give ear to my prayer, O God; and hide not thyself from my supplication" (Psalm 55:1). And, God heard David and comforted him and David uttered these words which are a comfort to us now, saying, "God is nigh unto all them that call upon Him in truth."

God is inescapable, and He is sovereign. Thus, individuals everywhere must recognize their dependence upon God. It is not necessary to assume a certain position or pose when one prays. But, certainly, it is fitting to kneel when seeking God in prayer, because such a position shows humility of spirit. St. Paul reminds us: "I bend my knees to the Father." But, he further said: "With every form of prayer and supplication you carry on prayer." Just as Jesus said to the disciples, "When you stand praying, forgive."

Hence, it is not the position that matters when an individual prays, because we can pray while we are doing our daily tasks with every step we take as long as God is ordering our steps.

We must understand that it is only the one true God who answers the prayers of His children, not the false gods of the world we might worship from time to time because God can "do more than super abundantly beyond all things, we can ask or conceive." Hence, God is able to hear the prayers of every individual and His power of perception being such that He is able to comprehend even our thoughts.

"O thou who hearest prayer, unto thee shall all flesh come." Since all flesh is imperfect and sinful, how can anyone approach a perfect and righteous God. The righteous must live by faith. The spiritual answer to eternal life is faith and obedience to God's will. For if you have an unshakeable faith in the existence of God and in His power and His willingness to aid those who seek His ways, and if you believe God is capable of fulfilling His promises regardless of how impossible they might seem from a human standpoint, then God counts this believer as righteous. God counts faith as righteousness because it is "faith" that pleases God.

When Jesus Christ came an entirely new avenue of prayer to God came into being when Jesus said: "No-one comes to God the Father except through me." Jesus further said: "If you ask anything in my name, I will in no wise refuse it." Jesus' disciples realized the importance of prayer and asked Him to teach them how to pray. Jesus gave the disciples instructions on how to pray that are indispensable even to this day. Jesus said to them: "And when you pray, thou shalt not be as the hypocrites are: for they love to pray standing in the synagogues and in the corners of the streets, that they may be seen of men. Verily I say unto you, they have their reward. But thou, when you prayest, enter into thy closet, and when thou hast shut the door, pray to thy Father which is in secret; and thy Father which seeth in secret shall reward thee openly" (Matthew 6:5-6). Jesus prayed not to give attention to Himself, but to give witness to the glory of God. Jesus also told His disciples, "When you pray do not say the same thing over and over again, for God your Father knows what you have need of even before you ask Him."

"After this manner therefore pray ye: Our Father which art in heaven, Hallowed be thy name. Thy kingdom come. Thy will be done in earth, as it is in heaven. Give us this day our daily bread. And forgive us our debts, as we forgive our debtors. And lead us not into temptation, but deliver us from evil. For thine is the Kingdom, and the power, and the glory forever. Amen." (Matthew 6:9-13).

America, allow me to warn you just as Elvis Presley did in his popularized song, "Don't Step On My Blue Suede Shoes," America needs to stop stepping on God's principles and think that God is going to continue to bless America! Thus, Christians, especially Christian Right Evangelicals, I am warning you to take your profession of the Christian religion (faith), seriously. Take Jesus Christ and the cross, seriously. Moreover, become serious about your prayer life, because it is time for us to pray for the soul of American society. In the 1990's, President Clinton popularized the slogan: "It's the economy, stupid." In 2016, Donald J. Trump vulgarized and demonized this concept. Now, American society is spiritually upside down, because "the love of money is the root of all evil: which while some coveted after, they have erred from the faith, and pierced themselves through with many sorrows" (1 Timothy 6:10).

President Trump spiritually and morally symbolizes everything that is wrong with American society, and at the same, while demonstrating that he has no spiritual-moral character as a leader, America may as well have elected a criminal-convict from the infamous "San Quinton Prison", for after all, President Trump does have a criminal mind Jesus's model prayer is unselfish in every spiritual respect. It has been rightly said that "prayer can only be effective when the individual feels the need to pray, and therefore, he is driven to pray about situations that he cannot control. Consequently, he bends his knees in humility, and he prays in sincerity, rather than in form and fashion; something that he has fallen into simply out of habit."

Yes, prayer is one of the most effective weapons that the Christian believer has because God is ever willing to hear the prayers of the faithful who seek to do His will, because He is our strength and our help in ages past, and above all, there is none other.

Now, more so than ever before, every American and especially Christians must take their prayer lives seriously. On a daily basis, as Christians, we must offer our lives up in service to God and others. Jesus always talked about a life to be lived in service to others, not just moralistic hypocrisy. In fact, Jesus talked about an inner life radically oriented toward outward obedience to the will of God. Blessed is the individual who has submitted to the spiritual discipline, divine-direction of God, and His will. Amen!

CONCLUSION

For Jesus, community is the unquestioned presupposition of human life. Jesus walked along the shores of the Galilee River calling men out of themselves and their occupations to form a community under the reality of God. Jesus had just been baptized by John the Baptist in the Jordan River, and for forty days and nights, he fasted in the wilderness. Immediately, after Jesus's baptismal experience, he began his ministry with a call: "Come follow me, and I will make you "fishers of men". The "Call" was about the "Great Commission". The men (Disciples) who followed Jesus formed a community: The Christian church.

Jesus was calling men to remake their lives and the "Call" was revolutionary in nature. In fact, it caused Andrew, and Simon Peter to deny their personal ambitions, repent, and follow Jesus. In speaking to the twelve disciples, Jesus spoke beyond them to future generations of individuals who would listen. For after all, listening is a godly quality. More importantly, the 'Call" of Jesus was about asking individuals to liberate themselves from selfishness. Each individual is responsible for his own life under God: "Must Jesus bear the Cross alone and the world goes free? No, there is a Cross for everyone". Without a doubt, sin causes separation from God, and this is why Jesus came to liberate us from the old sinful relationship with self to a new relationship with God and neighbor: "The Two Great Commandments of Jesus" (Matthew 22: 34-40).

The spiritual meaning of the "Call" is about Cross-bearing. In other words, to become a "fisher of men", individuals must have patience. Moreover, individuals must have perseverance that is never become discouraged, but always be willing to try, and try again. Individuals must have an eye for the "right moment", because there is a time to speak and a time to be silent. Hence, a wise person knows that some individuals will accept the Word of God and some will not, because you will win some, and you will lose some.

Christian brothers and sisters, pastoral leadership is all about teaching and preaching the unadulterated Word of God, in and out of season. Jesus never built a physical church building. The ministry of Jesus was oriented toward reconstructing lives in the Will of God. In fact, at one time, Jesus had an outdoor congregation of over 5,000.

Christians should always avoid worthless arguments, and the desire to become rich, but always and forever desire godliness. Pastoral leader(s) God has charged you to: "Preach the word; be instant in season, and out of season; reprove, rebuke, exhort with long suffering and doctrine. For the time will come when they will not endure sound doctrine; but after their own lusts shall they heap to themselves teachers, having itchy ears; and they shall turn away their ears from the truth, and shall be turned unto fables. But watch thou in all things, endure afflictions, do the work of an evangelist, make full proof of thy ministry." (2 Timothy 4: 1-5). In every sermon, God must WIN simply, because: "Thou art worthy, O Lord, to receive glory and honor and power: for thou hast created all things, and for thy pleasure they are and were created" (Revelation 4:11). AMEN!